Original title:
When I Held On

Copyright © 2024 Swan Charm
All rights reserved.

Author: Sara Säde
ISBN HARDBACK: 978-9916-89-721-8
ISBN PAPERBACK: 978-9916-89-722-5
ISBN EBOOK: 978-9916-89-723-2

BLOOD AND CIRCUSES

A FOOTBALL JOURNEY THROUGH
EUROPE'S REBEL REPUBLICS

BLOOD AND CIRCUSES

ROBERT O'CONNOR

Biteback Publishing

First published in Great Britain in 2020 by
Biteback Publishing Ltd
Westminster Tower
3 Albert Embankment
London SE1 7SP
Copyright © Robert O'Connor 2020

Robert O'Connor has asserted his right under the Copyright, Designs and Patents Act 1988 to be identified as the author of this work.

All rights reserved. No part of this publication may be reproduced, stored in a retrieval system or transmitted, in any form or by any means, without the publisher's prior permission in writing.

This book is sold subject to the condition that it shall not, by way of trade or otherwise, be lent, resold, hired out or otherwise circulated without the publisher's prior consent in any form of binding or cover other than that in which it is published and without a similar condition, including this condition, being imposed on the subsequent purchaser.

Every reasonable effort has been made to trace copyright holders of material reproduced in this book, but if any have been inadvertently overlooked the publisher would be glad to hear from them.

ISBN 978-1-78590-511-7

10 9 8 7 6 5 4 3 2 1

A CIP catalogue record for this book is available from the British Library.

Set in Times New Roman

Printed and bound in Great Britain by
CPI Group (UK) Ltd, Croydon CR0 4YY

The Strength Weaving Through Wounds

In the silence of night, grace flows,
Through cracks of despair, hope glows.
Hearts battered, yet not broken,
In every wound, love is spoken.

Hands reach for heaven's light,
Each scar becomes a guiding sight.
Strength woven from threads of pain,
In the storm, we rise again.

With every tear, faith ignites,
In shadows deep, God's love unites.
The tapestry of life we mend,
A journey of wounds that transcend.

Every struggle shapes our way,
In the darkest night, we pray.
Strength finds us in quiet dew,
In the heart's ache, love's light shines through.

With each heartbeat, we reclaim,
The power in Jesus' name.
Together, through wounds, we stand,
In His arms, we understand.

Heartstrings Tied to God's Will

In the morning light, we rise,
With heartstrings tied to love's skies.
Every whisper of His grace,
Brings peace to our sacred space.

Through trials that seek to entwine,
We find strength in the divine.
Prayers lift like gentle wings,
Carried forth, our spirit sings.

Even when shadows assail,
God's promise will never fail.
Ties of faith, woven so dear,
In every doubt, He is near.

Through struggles, His light glows bright,
Guiding us into the night.
With every heartbeat, we know,
In His hands, love will flow.

Faith's embrace, a warm cocoon,
Cradled there, we find our tune.
Together, our spirits entwine,
In God's will, forever shine.

The Resilience of Spirit

In the dust of trials faced,
The spirit rises, unchased.
Each burden becomes a seed,
In faith's garden, we succeed.

With every storm that beckons near,
Courage echoes, loud and clear.
The heart beats strong against the night,
In resilience, we find our light.

Mountains tremble, yet we stand,
Together, united, hand in hand.
Though waves crash with fierce delight,
In His love, we ignite.

From ashes, we learn to soar,
Finding strength in every core.
Through the tears, we paint our grace,
In His presence, we find our place.

With unwavering hope inside,
We lean on faith as our guide.
The spirit's fire, fiercely bright,
In every struggle, we find our fight.

Clinging to the Breath of Eternity

In the stillness, breath anew,
Clinging to the hope that's true.
Every moment, a precious gift,
In love's embrace, our spirits lift.

Through the valleys, we shall tread,
With faith as our daily bread.
Eternity whispers our name,
In each heartbeat, love's pure flame.

Time may tangle, yet we find,
The peace that comes from a faithful mind.
Moments stained with grace Divine,
Reveal paths where hearts align.

In the quiet of the soul,
Eternity makes us whole.
In His arms, we turn the key,
Clinging close, we will be free.

With each breath, a promise flows,
In every trial, love bestows.
Clinging tightly, fears take flight,
Eternity shines through the night.

The Covenant of Trust

In quiet reverence we stand,
Hand in hand, a sacred band.
In whispers soft, the promise flows,
A bond of faith that ever grows.

In trials faced, our hearts entwined,
With every prayer, our souls aligned.
Through storms that rage, we find our guide,
In love and light, we shall abide.

Each step we take, a vow renewed,
In service pure, our hearts imbued.
With every breath, a hope reborn,
In trust we walk, through night and morn.

With open hearts, we dare to dream,
In unity, we brightly beam.
A tapestry of grace we weave,
In this, our truth, we do believe.

Together bound, forever blessed,
In faith upheld, we find our rest.
In joy and pain, we lift our song,
In trust divine, we do belong.

Bound by Threads of Light

In shadows deep, a whisper calls,
A gentle light through heaven falls.
With every thread, a story spun,
In unity, we all are one.

Each heart aflame, a beacon bright,
In darkest times, we shine our light.
Together woven, dreams entwined,
In love's embrace, our souls aligned.

Through trials faced, we lift our hearts,
In every end, a new life starts.
With courage strong, we rise anew,
Bound by threads of love so true.

In sacred circles, we arise,
In gratitude, we open eyes.
With every word, a blessing shared,
In collective grace, we're fully bared.

In essence pure, we march along,
With every step, we sing our song.
Bound by threads of light above,
In harmony, we find our love.

A Heart Alight with Grace

Within the silence, still and deep,
A heart awakens from its sleep.
In tender moments, grace ignites,
In every dawn, the spirit fights.

With open hands, we seek to share,
A gift of love, a humble prayer.
Through every joy, in every tear,
A heart alight, for all to hear.

In acts of kindness, echoes rise,
In simple truths, the spirit flies.
In harmony, we tread the way,
For light and love shall rule the day.

With gentle faith, our visions bloom,
In sacred space, we cast away gloom.
In gratitude, we find our place,
In each embrace, a heart of grace.

Through every trial, the heart endures,
In every struggle, faith ensures.
A radiant soul, forever bright,
A heart alight with love's pure light.

In the Grotto of Serenity

In tranquil shade, the spirit rests,
Within the grotto's soft caress,
With every breath, the whispers flow,
In peace profound, our hearts do grow.

A gentle stream runs clear and bright,
Reflecting stars that grace the night.
In stillness found, we learn to see,
The sacred path that sets us free.

Each moment cherished, time stands still,
As nature speaks, and we fulfill.
In harmony, our souls take flight,
In the grotto's calm, we find our light.

With every sigh, the world recedes,
In unity, we plant the seeds.
Of love and hope, forever true,
In this embrace, we are renewed.

In the sacred space, we mend our hearts,
Where silence sings and wisdom starts.
In the grotto's grace, we come alive,
Through serenity, we shall thrive.

The Stillness within the Storm

In tempest's fury, calm resides,
A whispered prayer, where hope abides.
No raging waves can drown the light,
For peace is found in darkest night.

Amidst the clash of fierce despair,
A gentle hand assures it's there.
In every clash, a sacred sign,
Trust in the stillness, the heart aligns.

When chaos swirls, and doubts arise,
Lift up your gaze, behold the skies.
The storm may roar, yet spirits soar,
In quiet trust, we seek for more.

The eye of truth amidst the fray,
Guides weary souls who lose their way.
In holy hush, we find our strength,
Embrace the stillness, love's great length.

So in the storm, when fears do rise,
Let faith be shaped, and spirits wise.
For in the heart of every fight,
The stillness calls, and brings us light.

Faith's Firm Grasp

In shadows deep, where doubt may dwell,
A flicker bold begins to swell.
With every breath, a promise fair,
In faith's embrace, we feel the care.

When trials loom and visions blur,
A steadfast heart begins to stir.
With every step, a stronger hold,
In trust, the truth begins to unfold.

Through valleys low and mountains high,
Our spirits soar, we reach the sky.
With faith as guide, no fear can last,
In present grace, we hold steadfast.

In whispers soft, the Spirit speaks,
Through all our trials, our courage peaks.
With faith's firm grasp, we face the day,
In sacred trust, we find our way.

So let us stand, united strong,
In faith's embrace, we all belong.
With hearts entwined, and hope amassed,
We journey forth, our shadows passed.

Cradling the Divine Within

In every breath the Spirit flows,
A gentle warmth, where love bestows.
We cradle dreams, both grand and small,
The divine whispers, we heed the call.

Through silence deep, our souls ignite,
In sacred spaces, we find the light.
With open hearts, our truths align,
In spirit's dance, the divine we find.

Among the stars, in vast expanse,
We see the spark, we take the chance.
With each embrace, a holy thread,
A tapestry where love is bred.

The holy murmurs guide our sight,
In every shadow, we find our light.
With every touch, the sacred spins,
In cradled grace, the journey begins.

So nurture well this inner flame,
In quiet whispers, call the name.
With joy and peace, we let love in,
Embrace the divine that lies within.

The Unseen Path of Trust

In morning mist, the path unfolds,
Where faith and trust, in silence hold.
Each step we take, though unaware,
In unseen trails, the Spirit's care.

With heavy hearts, we wander far,
Yet each lost soul is guided by star.
Through winding roads and shadows cast,
In trust we find, the die is cast.

When storms arise and fears ensue,
Let courage rise and guide us through.
With every heartbeat, a truth unspooled,
In a sacred dance, our hearts are ruled.

Through valleys low and towers tall,
Trust weaves a net, to catch our fall.
In every challenge, grace untried,
The unseen path, where love abides.

So walk with faith, though dark may be,
In every step, you'll find the key.
For in the trust of hearts entwined,
The unseen path, love's light will find.

Pillars of Belief Rising High

In the silence of dawn's early light,
We gather our hope, our spirits in flight.
Each prayer a whisper, a promise to keep,
Pillars of faith where our hearts shall leap.

Through trials we walk, hand in hand,
Bound by grace in a sacred band.
The journey was fraught, yet we rise above,
With each step a testament, grounded in love.

Mountains may tremble, seas may roar,
Yet in this belief, we shall endure more.
The sun will shine forth, bright and clear,
Guiding our path, dispelling our fear.

In the quiet moments, reflection we seek,
Our souls intertwined, strong yet meek.
Pillars of belief, never shall we sway,
For in unity's shelter, we find our way.

The Weight of an Unseen Hand

In shadows deep, where doubts collide,
We feel the weight, but not the guide.
An unseen hand, gently it sways,
Leading us forth through life's tangled maze.

Amidst the chaos, where hearts may break,
This hand brings solace, a peace we take.
Though trials may blind us, we hold our ground,
In whispers of trust, our strength is found.

With every burden, a lesson bestowed,
The hand lifts us up, on this holy road.
In moments of weakness, we find our grace,
Through faith's embrace, we run our race.

So let us not falter, nor stray from the will,
For the weight of the hand brings purpose still.
With hearts wide open, we boldly stand tall,
In the silence of faith, we answer the call.

Stalwart Beneath the Stars

In the vast expanse of the midnight sky,
We stand as sentinels, hearts lifted high.
Beneath the stars, our spirits ignite,
With dreams intertwined in the cloak of night.

Each twinkling light, a story untold,
A testament of faith, in brilliance bold.
Through trials we wander, through darkness we roam,
Stalwart in spirit, we find our way home.

The universe whispers, its secrets revealed,
In moments of wonder, our hearts are healed.
United as one, in the stillness we share,
Stalwart beneath stars, we rise in prayer.

A bond woven tight through the celestial dance,
We embrace the mystery, surrender to chance.
In the light of the cosmos, our worries dissolve,
As we trust in the journey, our souls evolve.

Bonds Forged in Sacred Fire

In the flicker of flames, our spirits ignite,
Bonds forged in sacred, illuminating sight.
Through trials and triumphs, we stand side by side,
In the heart of the fire, our fears we confide.

Through shadows we venture, where light flickers low,
Each ember a promise, in warmth we grow.
With courage as fuel, we kindle the flame,
Bonds forged in sacred, calling our name.

The heat of the struggle, a crucible divine,
In the face of the storm, our spirits entwine.
Together we rise, unyielding in grace,
Facing the trials, our hearts embrace.

Each scar a reminder, each bruise a song,
In the dance of the flames, we find where we belong.
With love as our guide, we shall never tire,
For we are united in this sacred fire.

In the Quietude of Prayer

In the stillness, hearts do bend,
Whispers rise, where souls ascend.
In quietude, we find our peace,
In sacred silence, our burdens cease.

Hands uplifted, hopes do soar,
Faith ignited, forevermore.
Each breath a prayer, each sigh a plea,
In humble trust, we seek to be.

The Fabric of Spiritual Encounters

Threads of light in woven dreams,
Connections pulse like rivers' streams.
In every glance, a story shared,
In every touch, divine love bared.

Gathered here, we find our place,
In the dance of grace, we face.
A tapestry of souls entwined,
In sacred moments, love defined.

The Blessing in Letting Go

In surrender, strength is found,
Chains of worry fall to ground.
With open hands, we release the past,
Embrace the journey, free at last.

In the letting go, we find our way,
Trusting the dawn that brightens day.
Each tear a seed, each loss a gain,
In the quiet, peace remains.

The Strength of Faith Unveiled

In shadows deep, hope takes flight,
A beacon shines through darkest night.
With every challenge, faith grows bold,
In trials faced, our hearts consoled.

Stand with courage, hearts ablaze,
In every storm, sing heartfelt praise.
For in the struggle, grace appears,
In unwavering faith, we conquer fears.

The Tapestry of Belief

In the quiet whispers of the night,
Threads of faith intertwine with might.
Each soul a stitch, in colors bright,
Woven together, in His holy light.

Mountains may tremble, the storm may rise,
Yet steadfast hearts gaze toward the skies.
In trials we find the sacred ties,
Our tapestry sings as hope replies.

Every tear shed, a pearl of grace,
In the fabric of love, we find our place.
With every prayer, we seek His face,
A journey of faith, our hearts embrace.

We stand as one, in joy and strife,
Hand in hand, we cherish life.
With every heartbeat, His love is rife,
In unity, we hold the knife.

So weave your dreams into the night,
For in the darkness, shines the light.
Together we rise, taking flight,
In the tapestry of belief, we unite.

Holding the Essence of Hope

In the dawn's embrace, we seek our way,
Breath of life whispers, 'Come what may.'
Through trials deep, our spirits sway,
Hope is the guide that will not fray.

Every sunrise paints a canvas pure,
With colors of faith, we find our cure.
In shadows long, His love is sure,
Holding the essence, we shall endure.

With every heartbeat, dreams take flight,
Through darkest valleys, we'll find our light.
His gentle presence, a sacred sight,
In moments fragile, hearts feel right.

Through desert sands, to river streams,
Hope flows like water, in whispered dreams.
In every challenge, His mercy redeems,
We rise together, stitched at the seams.

In unity's strength, we rise above,
Holding the essence, guided by love.
Together we stand, blessed from above,
In the garden of faith, we find our dove.

The Strength in Vulnerability

In the quiet moments, we lay bare,
The weight of burdens, we courageously share.
In our fragility, a promise we wear,
Strength blooms from roots of honest care.

Courage lies deep, behind closed doors,
In brokenness, the spirit soars.
The heart finds solace, as the soul explores,
Vulnerability, where true love pours.

In the cracks of life, the light breaks through,
In shared confessions, we find what's true.
Each whisper of pain, a gift anew,
Strength in our weakness, the pathway grew.

He lifts our gaze from fear and plight,
In faithful embrace, we find our light.
Together we rise, united in fight,
With open hearts, we ignite the night.

So let us stand, in truth's embrace,
For in our flaws, we find His grace.
In vulnerability's spirit, we find our place,
Strength blossoms here, in sacred space.

A Vessel for His Light

In the still of dawn, we rise and pray,
He fills our hearts in a gentle way.
A vessel of love, in light we stay,
Guided by truth, we walk His way.

With open arms, the world we greet,
Each step we take, His love is sweet.
Purpose ignites, in every heartbeat,
A vessel we are, where mercy meets.

Through shadows cast, the flame still burns,
In trials encountered, the spirit yearns.
For every lesson, the heart returns,
A vessel of light, where the candle churns.

In our kindness, His grace is shown,
In acts of love, we're never alone.
With every challenge, the seeds are sown,
A vessel of hope, in Him we've grown.

So let it shine, this light divine,
Through every moment, His love align.
In each of us, the glory is thine,
A vessel for His light, forever we'll shine.

Illuminated by Divine Light

In the stillness of the dawn,
Heavenly rays begin to shine,
Guiding hearts that seek the way,
Awakening the soul divine.

Angels whisper gentle truths,
In the silence, love abounds,
Every shadow finds its light,
In the grace that knows no bounds.

Mountains bow and rivers sing,
All creation lifts its voice,
In the presence of His love,
Every heart has cause to rejoice.

Wisdom flows like fragrant oil,
Lubricating our weary lives,
In surrender, we find strength,
As our spirit gladly thrives.

With each heartbeat, we are called,
To walk the path of endless grace,
Illuminated by His love,
In His arms, we find our place.

The Tenderness of Offering

In humble prayer, we find our peace,
A moment of silence, hearts laid bare,
The sweetness of grace envelops all,
In the stillness, we feel His care.

Offering our burdens, we lay them down,
In the melody of hope we find,
Each whisper of love, pure and profound,
In the softness of spirit, intertwined.

Hands outstretched in service bright,
Gifts of kindness, joy, and light,
With gratitude we share our hearts,
For in giving, we find our might.

The tender threads of compassion weave,
A tapestry of grace sublime,
As we love, we truly believe,
In the sacred dance of time.

Our offerings, small yet divine,
With faith, they bloom like flowers rare,
In the garden of His embrace,
We flourish, nurtured by His care.

Echoes of Eternal Belief

In the quiet of the morning light,
Voices rise in sacred song,
Echoes of a timeless faith,
Where every soul can feel they belong.

Stories shared through ages past,
Resounding truth in every heart,
From prophets bold to humble saints,
Their teachings never drift apart.

Each prayer a ripple on the sea,
A call that reaches far and wide,
In unity we stand as one,
Divine love, our greatest guide.

When trials shadow paths we tread,
And doubts like dark clouds may ensue,
We'll call upon the strength within,
In hope, our spirits will renew.

Eternal belief, a beacon bright,
In His embrace, we find our sight,
With hearts aflame, we rise again,
For in His love, our spirits ignite.

Clinging to the Gospel Message

In the pages of ancient texts,
Wisdom flows like rivers wide,
In each verse, a call to love,
A promise in which we confide.

With every step upon this path,
We clutch the words that guide our way,
The gospel truth, our anchor firm,
In stormiest seas, we trust and pray.

With faith as our unwavering shield,
And hope, the light that breaks the night,
We stand united, hearts aflame,
Proclaiming His love, a wondrous sight.

In trials faced, our spirits soar,
For in His grasp, we find our peace,
Clinging tight to His loving Word,
Our burdens lift; our fears decrease.

Together, we embrace the call,
To live in truth, to share the light,
Clinging to the gospel message,
In unity, our hearts ignite.

Finding Solace in Sacred Space

In the chapel's hush, I seek,
Whispers of the soul, so meek.
Candles flicker, shadows play,
Guiding me through night and day.

Each prayer a soft, gentle plea,
A moment to just be, to see.
In stillness, the spirit flows,
A peace that only stillness knows.

The stained glass glows, colors blend,
Messages of love they send.
Beneath arching boughs, I stand,
A humble heart in sacred land.

In silence, I release my strife,
Finding meaning, breathing life.
Wrapped in warmth of grace divine,
A whisper of the heart, a sign.

Each moment here becomes a prayer,
In sacred space, I lay me bare.
Embraced by hope, my spirit soars,
In solitude, my heart restores.

The Strength to Trust in Shadows

In shadows deep, I find my way,
Through valleys dark, where fears may sway.
Yet in the night, a light will guide,
With faith, I trust, I will abide.

The whispered doubts may seek to reign,
But I hold close my heart's refrain.
Each step I take, a prayer I weave,
In shadows' midst, I shall believe.

A voice within, it softly calls,
To rise again, despite the falls.
For even when the night seems long,
In silent strength, I find my song.

The night's embrace may seem so tight,
Yet dawn will kiss away the night.
With every breath, I trust the unseen,
In shadows cast, the light does glean.

So here I stand, in faith's embrace,
Embracing fear with gentle grace.
From darkness blooms a strength so true,
Each shadow leads me back to You.

A Heart in Unbroken Prayer

With every breath, a prayer I sing,
In morning light, my heart takes wing.
Through trials faced, and joy divine,
In unbroken prayer, I intertwine.

The universe listens to heartbeats near,
In whispered hopes, I cast my fear.
Each moment spent in holy grace,
A sacred journey, a sacred space.

In joy and sorrow, I find my song,
In the quiet hush, where I belong.
As shadows pass and daylight flows,
My heart in prayer forever grows.

With gratitude for lessons learned,
In the fires of faith, my spirit burned.
Each tear a token of love displayed,
In unbroken prayer, I am remade.

Every word a thread divine,
In a tapestry of love, I find.
United all, in heart and soul,
Unbroken prayer will make me whole.

The Glimmer of Eternal Flame

In the still of night, a flame does glow,
Eternal light, where love will flow.
A beacon bright, through dark's embrace,
The glimmer shines, a holy grace.

Through trials faced, and moments rare,
Each flicker whispers, You are there.
In every heart, this spark remains,
A sacred bond, through joy and pains.

The warmth surrounds, fears fade away,
In every night, awaits the day.
A tapestry of hope displayed,
In eternal flame, our fears are laid.

Together we find strength anew,
In glimmers shared, in hearts so true.
With every breath, we fan the spark,
A guiding light through shadows dark.

In moments lost, the flame will guide,
With faith anew, I will abide.
Each heart aglow, in love's own name,
Together we rise, in eternal flame.

A Journey Anchored in Light

In the stillness of dawn's embrace,
We wander, guided by faith's grace.
Each step unfolds a sacred space,
Where love and mercy interlace.

Through valleys low and mountains high,
We seek the truth and lift our eye.
With every breath, a fervent sigh,
Our spirits soar, we learn to fly.

In whispers soft, the heart will find,
The light that heals, the ties that bind.
In unity, our souls aligned,
A tapestry of love designed.

And though the road may shift and sway,
We trust the path, come what may.
For in His light, we find the way,
To brighter dawns, the hopes of day.

So let our journey thus unfold,
With hearts of courage, brave and bold.
In every moment, truth retold,
Anchored in light, we break the mold.

The Vessel of Renewed Strength

In the midst of trials fierce and wild,
Our spirits weary, but not defiled.
The vessel holds a strength deep-styled,
A promise of hope, a loving child.

With every storm that shakes our boats,
We find the grace that gently coats.
In unity, our faith promotes,
The whispers of peace, the heart's sweet notes.

With hands uplifted, we seek the light,
A refuge strong, our guiding delight.
Each tear we shed ignites the night,
And turns our burdens into flight.

So let us gather, strong and sure,
In every heart, a love so pure.
With faith, our spirits will endure,
As vessels filled, forever secure.

With every breath, we rise anew,
In strength unified, our path we strew.
A bond unbreakable, pure and true,
The vessel of strength, forever in view.

Embracing the Shattered Light

In fragments bright, our spirits gleam,
A dance of shadows, a radiant dream.
The broken pieces, a sacred theme,
Where love is stitched in every seam.

We gather light from every source,
Transforming pain into a force.
In shattered moments, we find our course,
Awakening souls, a divine endorsement.

With open arms, we hold the fire,
Each spark ignites a fierce desire.
In unity, we lift higher,
The light within, a boundless choir.

As storms may rage and darkness close,
We find the strength that softly grows.
In every heart, a garden sows,
The promise of peace when chaos goes.

So let us cherish the light we gain,
In shattered dreams, we feel the pain.
Yet in each crack, a chance to reign,
Embracing light, a love unchained.

Clutching Threads of Grace

In twilight's hush, we stand as one,
Clutching threads of grace, our work begun.
Each whispered prayer, a golden sun,
    Illuminates the race we run.

Through valleys deep and mountains steep,
  We bind our hearts, a promise to keep.
    In every loss, we learn to leap,
  The wisdom found in silence deep.

As lives entwined, our hopes will soar,
  In shared embrace, we find the core.
With courage strong, we seek for more,
    The threads of grace, forevermore.

So when the shadows loom and creep,
  We lift our voices, our souls to steep.
    In unity, the blessings seep,
Clutching grace, our hearts will leap.

For in each moment's gentle throng,
We find the notes of life's sweet song.
With threads of grace, we all belong,
    Together, we will rise, be strong.

In the Embrace of Faith

In the quiet dawn, I find my way,
Guided by light, the heart's gentle sway.
Each step a prayer, my soul takes flight,
In the embrace of faith, I find my might.

Through valleys deep and mountains high,
With open arms, the heavens reply.
In trials faced, I seek Your grace,
In the embrace of faith, I find my place.

Whispers of hope in shadows fall,
With every heartbeat, I heed the call.
Through doubts and fears, I rise anew,
In the embrace of faith, I cling to You.

The stars above, they softly sing,
Testimonies sweet of Your offering.
In every tear, a spark of trust,
In the embrace of faith, my spirit must.

I walk the path where angels tread,
In Your promise true, I've freely bled.
Forever anchored, my heart shall stay,
In the embrace of faith, come what may.

The Anchor in the Storm

When thunder roars and fierce winds blow,
I find my peace, Your love will show.
Through tempest tides, I hold on tight,
You are my anchor, my guiding light.

Each wave may crash, each fear may rise,
Yet in Your presence, I see the skies.
A steadfast rock amidst the fray,
You are my anchor, I kneel and pray.

In darkest nights, when shadows creep,
Your whispered words bring strength to keep.
No fear can quell this faith inside,
You are my anchor, my daily guide.

With every trial, my heart will trust,
In Your embrace, I rise from dust.
For every storm shall pass away,
You are my anchor, my hopes replay.

So grant me courage, let me soar,
With You beside, I ask for more.
In every tempest, I'll safely roam,
You are my anchor, my eternal home.

Beneath Celestial Wings

In morning light, I lift my gaze,
Beneath celestial wings, Your love displays.
Guided by whispers from realms above,
I walk in grace, wrapped in Your love.

Each gentle breeze carries Your tune,
While stars shine bright beneath the moon.
In silence deep, Your presence sings,
I trust my soul beneath celestial wings.

When burdens weigh and shadows loom,
I find solace in the sacred room.
With open heart, my spirit clings,
I rest in peace beneath celestial wings.

Through valleys low and mountains steep,
Your promise keeps me from the deep.
In every moment, Your light springs,
I soar on high beneath celestial wings.

Forever cradled, my heart shall sing,
In every joy, the comfort brings.
With every breath, my spirit flings,
To dance with faith beneath celestial wings.

Whispered Prayers in Silence

In tranquil hours, my heart performs,
A symphony of whispered forms.
With each soft breath, my spirit plays,
Whispered prayers in silence raise.

The world around may fade away,
In quiet moments, I choose to stay.
In whispered thoughts, Your light estranges,
The shadows cast, the heart rearranges.

Each prayer a thread, spun from the heart,
Binding my soul to love's own art.
In stillness found, Your peace engages,
Whispered prayers in silence stages.

Through trials faced and fears beguiled,
I seek the warmth of love's sweet smile.
With faith renewed, my spirit changes,
Embraced in hope, whispered prayers in silence.

So lift my voice, though soft and meek,
In trust, I find the strength I seek.
For in the silence, my heart engages,
The sacred truth of whispered prayers in silence.

The Unbreakable Thread

In shadows deep, a light remains,
A thread of hope through winding pains.
With faith we weave our hearts anew,
A bond unbroken, strong and true.

Through trials faced, our spirits soar,
Each knot a tale, forevermore.
In unity, we rise and stand,
Together bound by His sweet hand.

The fabric of our prayers entwined,
With whispers soft, the heart aligned.
His guidance flows like rivers wide,
In every storm, He is our guide.

The thread of love that never frays,
In darkest nights, it brightly plays.
A tapestry of grace we find,
In every soul, His light defined.

With threads of mercy, stitched with care,
A garment woven, rich and rare.
In every moment, let us tread,
Upon this path, the unbreakable thread.

In the Hands of Providence

In stillness found, the heart does rest,
With every beat, His love expressed.
In hands unseen, we trust our way,
Through trials faced, both night and day.

The gentle whisper guides our path,
In storms of life, we find His wrath.
Yet in His arms, we seek our peace,
In every struggle, finding ease.

Each moment woven, purpose clear,
A tapestry of hope held dear.
In plans divine, we find our role,
The hands of fate that rock the soul.

With every tear, a lesson learned,\nA flame of faith,
within us burned.
In quiet prayer, we find our strength,
In His embrace, we go the length.

In grateful hearts, we lift our song,
With faith unyielding, we belong.
In the hands of Providence we see,
A future bright, He holds the key.

The Promise of Dawn

As night gives way to morning light,
Hope awakens from the night.
With each new dawn, a chance to start,
A promised gift to every heart.

The sun ascends, a golden ray,
In silence breaks the dark dismay.
His love, a beacon shining bright,
Guides weary souls towards the light.

The promise whispered on the breeze,
A gentle call to minds at ease.
In every flower, in every song,
The dawn reminds us we belong.

With every breath, our hearts renew,
In woven dreams, we see Him true.
For in each dawn, a chance to strive,
To live and love, to truly thrive.

Embrace the light, let shadows flee,
In the sunrise, we are free.
The promise of dawn, forever near,
In every heart, His love sincere.

The Chalice of Divine Love

In a sacred cup, our hearts will pour,
The sweetest nectar, forevermore.
With every sip, His grace we feel,
A love divine, His hearts reveal.

The chalice holds our hopes and dreams,
In its embrace, we find the seams.
Each drop a blessing, rich and pure,
In faith, a bond, we shall endure.

With every taste, our spirits rise,
In unity, we touch the skies.
The divine love flows from us to him,
A river full, not bound by sin.

In humble hearts, we lift the glass,
To celebrate the moments passed.
For in this chalice, life is shared,
The love of God, forever bared.

Let every soul partake and sing,
Of love bestowed, our offering.
In the chalice of divine embrace,
We find our home, we touch His grace.

The Dance of Faith Amidst Trials

In the shadows where doubts reside,
Faith takes the lead, our gentle guide.
With every step, we rise and fall,
The heart beats louder, answering the call.

When storms surround and hope feels thin,
We find our strength deep within.
Held by grace that will not fade,
Through trials, our spirits cascade.

The dance of trust ignites the soul,
Whirling in rhythm, we become whole.
With eyes uplifted to the skies,
We find our purpose and never disguise.

In moments lost, we seek the light,
Faith's embrace is our sacred rite.
Through every challenge, joy and strife,
We move with love, the dance of life.

In the silence, His whispers speak,
A promise full, the strong and weak.
Together we sway, come what may,
In the dance of faith, we find our way.

Cradled by Celestial Assurance

In the cradle of night, stars shine bright,
 They whisper secrets of divine light.
 With every twinkle, our spirits soar,
  Cradled by hope forevermore.

When burdens weigh and shadows creep,
 We find solace in dreams so deep.
 The gentle touch of celestial grace,
 Wraps us in love's warm embrace.

Each tear we shed, a prayer unspoken,
In quiet moments, our hearts are broken.
 Yet from the ashes, new life begins,
  With every trial, our spirit wins.

In the vastness of the sky so wide,
 We walk unafraid, with Him beside.
 Together we rise, no longer alone,
Cradled in faith, our hearts have grown.

As dawn breaks forth, the shadows flee,
 In the light of love, we are free.
 Celestial assurance guides our way,
 In every heartbeat, we find our stay.

In the Presence of Infinite Hope

In the quiet hush of the dawn light,
Hope blooms softly, a beautiful sight.
With every heartbeat, a promise is made,
In the presence of hope, fears begin to fade.

When the world feels heavy, and courage wanes,
We find strength in prayer, despite our chains.
With hands uplifted, we lift our voice,
In the presence of hope, we rejoice.

Whispers of promise reach out to us,
A gentle nudge, a holy trust.
Each moment a gift, every breath divine,
In the presence of hope, our spirits align.

Through valleys of shadow and mountains high,
We hold on to dreams, we spread our wings to fly.
Together we journey, hand in hand,
In the presence of hope, we boldly stand.

Let faith be our anchor, love be our guide,
In the presence of hope, we shall abide.
With hearts wide open, we embrace the day,
For in hope's embrace, we find our way.

The Bridge of Unshakeable Love

Across the river of grief and pain,
Stands a bridge where love shall reign.
With every heartbeat, we build it strong,
A sanctuary where we all belong.

Through trials faced, hand in hand,
We walk together on this land.
Unshakeable love, our guiding light,
Illuminates darkness, chases the night.

Each soul a thread in the fabric we weave,
Embracing the lost, the raw, and the grieved.
In laughter and tears, joy intertwined,
On this bridge of love, our hearts aligned.

Every step taken, with faith as our breath,
We conquer the shadows, defying all death.
For love is the bond that shall not let go,
The bridge that we walk, where seeds of hope grow.

When storms may rage and winds howl loud,
We find our strength, steadfast, and proud.
For together we stand, come what may,
On the bridge of unshakeable love, we stay.

A Testament of Unseen Fortitude

In shadows deep, faith does arise,
A whisper soft, a strength that lies.
Through trials faced, we find our way,
In prayerful hearts, we choose to stay.

With every breath, the spirit lifts,
In quietude, we find our gifts.
Trusting the path, though dark it seems,
A testament born of fervent dreams.

When burdens heavy make us bend,
The light within will not descend.
For in His grace, we stand so tall,
Unseen fortitude guides us through all.

Through storm and fire, we shall persevere,
For love divine will calm all fear.
A sacred bond can never break,
United hearts find strength to make.

In unity, we lift each prayer,
Emboldened souls, our burdens share.
A testament of hearts so pure,
In unseen fortitude, we endure.

Silence Cradled in Sacred Space

In sacred stillness, hearts align,
The hush of time, a gift divine.
With each soft breath, the world fades away,
In silence cradled, we choose to stay.

Beneath the stars, our spirits sing,
A quiet hope, like spring's first wing.
The echoes of the past, they cease,
In sacred space, we find our peace.

The whispers of the heart unfold,
A silent truth, more precious than gold.
In this embrace, we trust, we know,
That grace shall always gently flow.

With open hearts, we learn to listen,
In flowing light, our souls glisten.
For in the quiet, love does grow,
A sacred dance in ebb and flow.

In every still, a presence near,
The pulse of faith, forever clear.
In silence cradled, we find our way,
In sacred embrace, we choose to stay.

In the Twilight of Holding Firm

As daylight wanes, we stand in grace,
In twilight's glow, we find our place.
With steadfast hearts, we hold the line,
A promise made, through love divine.

In whispered prayers, our hopes are sown,
Through darkened paths, we walk alone.
Yet in the stillness, spirits soar,
In twilight's hold, we seek for more.

For love endures, and faith will shine,
An anchor set in hearts entwined.
Through trials faced beneath the sun,
In the twilight, we become one.

With open hands, we greet the night,
The stars our guide, celestial light.
In shadows cast, our truth remains,
In holding firm, love breaks all chains.

In every breath, resilience grows,
A steadfast heart, through highs and lows.
In twilight's grasp, we rise anew,
In holding firm, we find what's true.

An Embrace Beyond This World

In gentle grace, creation sighs,
An embrace felt through the skies.
With hearts that seek, though far apart,
We find the thread that binds the heart.

From earth to heaven, a journey made,
In love's embrace, our fears allayed.
For in the depths of every soul,
An echo calls, a sacred goal.

Through trials faced, we rise and meet,
In every challenge, love's heartbeat.
An embrace beyond what eyes can see,
A whisper soft, a symphony.

In every tear, a story flows,
In every laugh, joy softly grows.
For in this bond, no line divides,
An embrace felt where love resides.

When earthly ties begin to fray,
An embrace eternal leads the way.
Through realms unknown, we find our home,
In love's embrace, we are not alone.

Through Tempests and Trials We Stand

In storms that roar, we find our grace,
Through trials tough, we seek Your face.
With faith as shield, we hold our ground,
In darkest nights, Your love is found.

The winds may howl, the waves may crash,
Yet in Your light, our fears we quash.
Hands lifted high, we shall endure,
In every struggle, You are sure.

Though shadows loom, and doubts arise,
Your gentle whispers calm our sighs.
With hearts aflame, we rise again,
In every moment, You remain.

Through tempests fierce, we walk in trust,
Your promises, our hope's robust.
In every trial, You are our guide,
With You, dear Lord, we abide.

So let the storms and trials come,
In battles fought, we stand as one.
With faith, we light the darkest night,
Through tempests wild, You are our might.

Embracing the Divine Presence

In silent prayer, we seek Your grace,
In every moment, we find our place.
With open hearts, we receive the light,
Embracing You, our guiding sight.

In every breath, Your love is near,
Through joy and pain, we persevere.
With gratitude, we lift our song,
In Your embrace, we all belong.

Though shadows creep and fears surround,
In faith, we stand on sacred ground.
Your presence strong, a sweet refrain,
In every loss, You hold our pain.

As day breaks forth and night falls down,
In quiet trust, our hearts are found.
Each moment shared, a treasure vast,
In Your divine, we are steadfast.

So let us walk, hand in hand with grace,
In every trial, we seek Your face.
With love as armor, we go forth,
Embracing You, our sacred source.

The Quiet Power of Surrender

In stillness lies our greatest strength,
In letting go, we find the length.
With open hearts, we earn our peace,
In quiet power, we find release.

As burdens lift and worries fade,
In surrender, our fears are laid.
With trust in You, we cease to strive,
In gentle calm, our spirits thrive.

Though tempests rage and doubts appear,
In trust, we draw Your presence near.
With every breath, we feel the flow,
In sacred silence, our faith will grow.

Through trials faced, we learn to bend,
In yielding hearts, we find the end.
With love as guide, we flow like streams,
In quiet moments, we find our dreams.

So let us rest in love's embrace,
In every heartache, every grace.
With faith we stand, in You we trust,
The quiet power, in You, is just.

As Storms Collide in Silent Reflection

As thunder roars and lightning strikes,
In silent prayer, our heart unites.
With every clash, we search for peace,
In sacred stillness, doubts release.

The skies may darken, fears may swell,
Yet in Your presence, all is well.
With reflective eyes, we see Your hand,
In every storm, we learn to stand.

As chaos reigns and tempests rise,
In faith, we breathe and lift our eyes.
With love our anchor, we embrace,
In every trial, we find Your grace.

Though storms may clash and shadows fall,
In quiet moments, we hear Your call.
With hearts attuned to love's refrain,
In silent reflection, peace we gain.

Through every trial and every night,
In faith's embrace, we find the light.
With courage strong, we face the fight,
As storms collide, Your love ignites.

The Warmth of an Open Heart

In kindness, where love begins to bloom,
Compassion whispers, easing the gloom.
Hearts embrace, in gentle grace,
As warmth unfolds in this sacred space.

With arms wide open, we share our light,
Bridging the distance, banishing night.
In every smile, a spark ignites,
Forging a bond that forever delights.

Through trials faced, together we stand,
In unity's glow, we lend a hand.
The warmth of hope, our guiding flame,
In the name of love, we lift His name.

Let patience reign, as seasons shift,
With faith as our anchor, love is a gift.
Through laughter and tears, we journey on,
In the heart's embrace, we are never alone.

As the sun rises, illuminating the day,
We walk together, come what may.
The warmth of an open heart does shine,
In peace and harmony, our souls entwine.

The Trusting Journey Through Shadows

In shadows cast where fears may creep,
We hold our faith, our promise to keep.
Each step we take, though rough and steep,
Guided by grace, we rise from sleep.

A trusting heart, a beacon bright,
Illuminates the path in the night.
With every heartbeat, courage is sown,
In the depths of darkness, we're never alone.

Through doubts that whisper, we find our way,
In silence and stillness, we choose to pray.
With open hands, we release control,
Embracing the journey that shapes our soul.

During the trials, we learn to bend,
In brokenness, our hearts can mend.
With every stumble, we learn to fly,
On wings of faith, we reach for the sky.

As the dawn breaks, hope takes the lead,
Trusting the journey, we plant the seed.
In shadows we wander, but never despair,
For love's gentle light is always there.

Conduits of Sacred Spirit

In every breath, the Spirit flows,
Through sacred whispers, love bestows.
Each heart a vessel, carrying grace,
In the dance of life, we find our place.

Through trials faced, we learn to see,
The threads of unity in you and me.
In moments shared, we rise and bind,
Conduits of spirit, eternally entwined.

In the quiet dawn, His presence calls,
Through every challenge, His mercy falls.
With every tear, a prayer ascends,
The sacred bond that never ends.

Together we walk this hallowed ground,
In gratitude's song, our hearts resound.
With open hands, we share the light,
As conduits of spirit, we shine so bright.

In sacred stillness, our souls are one,
Through love's embrace, we've just begun.
Wherever we journey, we're never apart,
Bound by the echoes of the sacred heart.

The Graceful Hold of Faith

In silent moments, faith takes hold,
A gentle whisper, stories untold.
With every breath, we're cradled near,
In the grace of love, we conquer fear.

Through valleys deep, our spirits rise,
Guided by the light from the skies.
With hands united, we walk this road,
In the graceful hold, we share the load.

In darkest nights, hope will ignite,
A beacon bright, our guiding light.
Through every storm, we stand as one,
With faith's embrace, all battles won.

As petals fall, new blooms appear,
The cycle of life, a truth held dear.
With open hearts, we journey far,
In the graceful hold, we find who we are.

So let us trust in the unseen way,
In every heartbeat, grace will stay.
In faith we flourish, in love we soar,
In the graceful hold, forevermore.

The Light Beyond the Grasp

In shadows deep, a beacon glows,
A guiding hand where faith bestows.
Through trials faced, we seek the flame,
A love divine, forever the same.

With every step on paths unknown,
The whispers of the heart are sown.
In silence still, we find His grace,
A light that time cannot erase.

When burdens weigh on weary souls,
His promise shines, it makes us whole.
Through darkest nights, hope pierces through,
A radiant dawn breaks anew.

In every prayer a seed of peace,
A faith that loves will never cease.
With open hearts, we stand in awe,
Of mysteries held in sacred law.

So let us walk where spirit guides,
Embracing all that love abides.
For in the light beyond the grasp,
Eternal truth in arms we clasp.

Echoes of a Steadfast Heart

In gentle tones, the spirit calls,
A steady voice that never falls.
Through storms of doubt, it carries near,
The echoes of a heart sincere.

With every heartbeat, truth resounds,
A melody that knows no bounds.
In stillness found, we catch the sound,
Of faith renewed, on holy ground.

As shadows fade and daylight breaks,
The steadfast heart, in love, awakes.
With open hands, we share the grace,
In every moment, His embrace.

In every trial, His strength we see,
A woven thread of destiny.
In unity, our voices rise,
To sing His praise beyond the skies.

So let us hold to what is true,
With every breath, we start anew.
For in the echoes, hearts shall find,
The boundless love of the divine.

Embracing the Eternal Whisper

A quiet breeze through ancient trees,
Speaks of love that sets us free.
In whispers soft, the spirit sways,
And guides us through our earthly days.

With hearts attuned to sacred sound,
In every moment, grace abounds.
We feel His presence, near and clear,
With every breath, the truth we hear.

Time may fade, but love remains,
A gentle strength in joys and pains.
Through trials faced and paths we roam,
His whispered words will lead us home.

In nature's song, we find our peace,
A sacred dance that will not cease.
We hold the light, we feel the flame,
In eternal whispers, know His name.

So let us gather, hearts entwined,
In every soul, His love defined.
For in the silence, loud and clear,
We hear the call, forever near.

Chains of Love Unbroken

In trials faced and burdens shared,
A bond of love, so deeply cared.
Through every storm and weary night,
We find our strength in shared light.

With hands that lift and hearts that bind,
Together in grace, each soul aligned.
For in our trials, love finds a way,
A chain unbroken, come what may.

In laughter shared, in tears that fall,
The threads of hope connect us all.
As mercy flows and kindness grows,
The chain of love forever glows.

With every heart that joins the plight,
In unity, we shine so bright.
So let us cherish what we hold,
The stories of our hearts unfold.

For in this journey, near or far,
Love lights our path, a guiding star.
No length too great, no distance bold,
The chains of love, forever gold.

In the Sanctuary of Remaining

In hallowed halls where silence dwells,
God's whispers weave through ancient bells.
In stillness, souls find grace anew,
As light breaks forth, revealing truth.

With every breath, the angels sing,
A tapestry of hope they bring.
In shadows cast, His love remains,
Cleansing hearts of every strain.

Through trials faced, we stand in prayer,
In the sanctuary, we lay bare.
With faithful hands, we lift our cries,
As faith ascends, and fear defies.

In moments lost, His presence found,
Upon the earth, our spirits bound.
Through every tear, a lesson brought,
In trusting arms, we are sought.

So here we'll wait, in hope profound,
For in His love, our peace is found.
In the sanctuary, hearts align,
With grace and mercy, we entwine.

A Heart Resilient in Prayer

In trembling hands, we lift our plea,
A heart resilient, set free.
With every whisper, grace unfolds,
In sacred silence, truth upholds.

Through darkest nights, the dawn will break,
Our spirits rise, for Christ's own sake.
With fervent prayer, we seek His face,
In humble hearts, we find our place.

Through trials deep, our faith remains,
In love's embrace, we shed our chains.
With steadfast hope, we march as one,
For in His light, we are never done.

O heart of mine, resilient be,
In prayer, we find the key.
When clouds arise and shadows fall,
In faith, we rise and heed the call.

With every step, our journey clear,
In trust, we cast away our fear.
In prayer, our spirits intertwine,
Resilient hearts, forever shine.

The Echoes of Unbroken Faith

In valleys low, where shadows loom,
The echoes call, dispelling gloom.
In whispers faint, their strength astounds,
Through trials faced, our hope rebounds.

Unbroken faith, a timeless thread,
Through storms and trials, we have tread.
In every heart, a courage grown,
Together, we are never alone.

With every prayer, an anchor strong,
In melodies of grace, we belong.
Through whispered doubts, His love resounds,
In faith unshaken, joy surrounds.

With open hearts, we seek the light,
In faith, we stand, prepared to fight.
With voices raised, our hymns declare,
In every moment, His love, we share.

In echoes clear, our spirits rise,
In steadfast hope, we touch the skies.
For unbroken faith will always stand,
A guiding light, a faithful hand.

The Flame that Guides the Faint of Heart

Amidst the storm, a gentle glow,
A flame that warms, a love to show.
To wanderers lost, it lights the way,
In darkest nights, it will not sway.

Through fear and doubt, the faint of heart,
Will find their strength, a brand new start.
For in His flame, our fears dissolve,
In love's embrace, our hearts evolve.

With every spark, a promise made,
In trials faced, we've not yet faded.
For hope ignites, our spirits soar,
In faith and love, we search for more.

Through whispered prayers, the flame expands,
A beacon bright, in weary lands.
With kindred souls, we gather 'round,
In warmth and grace, our truths are found.

So let that flame forever shine,
To guide our paths, our hearts entwine.
For in the light, we're never apart,
The flame that guides the faint of heart.

A Melody of Faithful Endurance

In shadows deep, we find our song,
With every breath, we march along.
Through trials fierce, our spirits rise,
With whispered prayers that touch the skies.

The road may twist, but still we stand,
In faith we forge, with guiding hand.
Each step we take, a bond renewed,
In grace, our hearts in worship stewed.

When storms may strike, and hope may fade,
We cling to love, our fears betrayed.
In every tear, a promise shines,
In every loss, the grace defined.

With steadfast hearts, we carry light,
In sacred truth, we find our sight.
Our voices raised in sweet refrain,
A melody that breaks the chain.

Through trials faced, together we rise,
In every breath, His grace supplies.
In faithful hearts, we sing His praise,
A timeless tune in endless days.

The Tree of Hope in Desolation

In barren lands, where shadows creep,
A tree of hope begins to weep.
Its branches reach towards the sun,
In quiet strength, the fight begun.

Roots delve deep in soil of sorrow,
In faith, they seek a brighter tomorrow.
With every leaf, a whispered prayer,
In every rustle, love laid bare.

Though winds may howl, and storms may break,
The tree stands firm, for love's own sake.
In stillness found, its heart beats strong,
A sanctuary where souls belong.

In twilight's glow, the branches sway,
Reminding us of the sacred way.
For in the dark, His light shall shine,
A beacon bright, forever mine.

Through trials faced, the roots grow strong,
In prayer, we find where we belong.
Together bound, in faith we'll stand,
A tree of hope in God's own hand.

The Weight of Holy Assurance

When burdens press, and spirits tire,
We seek the peace that lifts us higher.
In silence deep, we find our rest,
In holy assurance, we are blessed.

Each doubt may linger, clouds may form,
But faith ignites the spirit warm.
With every sigh, a promise claims,
In every heart, we call His name.

Though trials come like tides of night,
In His embrace, we find the light.
With gentle hands, He holds our fears,
In sacred trust, He dries our tears.

The weight of life may pull us low,
Yet in His love, we learn to grow.
With every step, His grace surrounds,
A melody in holy sounds.

In every storm, His peace shall reign,
Through every loss, we grasp what's plain.
The weight of holy love shall see,
In every heart, a legacy.

Reaching for the Sacred Embrace

In quiet nights, we lift our eyes,
Reaching for love beyond the skies.
With open hearts, we seek His face,
In every moment, His warm embrace.

Though trials come like waves on shore,
We stand in faith, and ask for more.
With every breath, our spirits stretch,
To grasp the grace that love shall etch.

In solitude, we feel His breath,
A sacred promise over death.
Though fears may rise, we shall not fall,
For in His arms, we hear the call.

The world may change, but He remains,
In every joy, He breaks the chains.
From pain to hope, our souls ascend,
In every heart, He is our friend.

In trust we rise, our hands held high,
Reaching for heavens in the sky.
In sacred hope, our spirits dance,
Embraced by love, we find our chance.

Gathering Fragments of Faith

In the silence of the night, we pray,
Whispers of hope, guiding the way.
Hearts united, in search of light,
Finding strength in every plight.

In every tear, His grace we find,
Pieces of love, intertwined.
A tapestry woven, thread by thread,
In the arms of faith, we are led.

Through trials faced, we rise again,
A chorus of trust, free from sin.
Each fragment a jewel, shining bright,
Together we stand, in divine sight.

With every breath, we seek His face,
In the quiet moments, we find grace.
Gathered in spirit, a sacred throng,
Holding each other, where we belong.

Let the pieces of our hearts align,
In love's embrace, we intertwine.
Through darkest storms, our light will shine,
In gathering faith, forever we bind.

The Divine Embrace of Tomorrow

In dawn's first light, a promise grows,
Hope blooms softly, as wisdom flows.
Each day a canvas, pure and bright,
We trust in the day, we walk in light.

With faith as our guide, we venture forth,
Seeking the treasures of heavenly worth.
In every heart, a song to sing,
Tomorrow awaits, with love to bring.

The shadows may linger, yet we press on,
Holding the dreams that dance at dawn.
With eyes of grace, we start anew,
In the embrace of divinity, we grew.

Through trials faced, our spirits soar,
In unity, we find the core.
Embraced by love, we take our stand,
Bound together, hand in hand.

Let not fear mark the road we tread,
For in faith's embrace, we are led.
With every heartbeat, a vow we make,
To rise and shine, for tomorrow's sake.

Loving Beyond the Abyss

In depths unseen, where shadows creep,
Our love is stronger, our promise deep.
Though valleys dark may call our name,
In the heart of faith, we are the same.

With every step that leads us near,
We find the light that calms our fear.
Through trials forged in flames of trust,
We rise anew, in love we must.

Together we journey, hand in hand,
Beyond the chasm, we make our stand.
A lighthouse beacon, guiding true,
In love's embrace, we're born anew.

With whispers soft, we heal the pain,
In sacred patience, peace we gain.
Beyond the abyss, hope gleams bright,
In loving hearts, we find our light.

So let the darkness come and go,
For in our bond, we always grow.
Through valleys low, our spirits sing,
Loving beyond the abyss, we cling.

A Sanctuary in Shadows

In the quiet dusk, where shadows dwell,
Whispers of solace, our hearts compel.
Sheltered in grace, we find our rest,
In the arms of love, we are blessed.

Each moment a prayer, softly spoken,
In trials faced, our spirits woken.
Through stormy nights, we seek the light,
In shadows cast, our love ignites.

With every heartbeat, a sacred vow,
To stand together, here and now.
In the refuge of faith, we find our peace,
In a sanctuary, fears release.

Through every storm, we hold on tight,
Guided by truth, we ascend the height.
In darkness, we shine, our bond so strong,
A sanctuary where we belong.

Let fears be still, as dawn's light breaks,
For in love's shelter, our spirit wakes.
In life's embrace, with faith we tread,
In shadows' sanctuary, love is spread.

The Sacred Bond of Resilience

In the heart of shadows deep,
Faith whispers secrets, truths to keep.
Each trial, a forge, each tear, a sign,
Bound in the spirit, our souls align.

With every step on rugged ground,
In unity's strength, hope is found.
Mountains may rise, storms may roar,
Yet hearts intertwined will endure evermore.

The path is steep, the night is long,
Together we rise, together we're strong.
In dawn's embrace, despair will flee,
The sacred bond our destiny.

Holding fast to love's sweet call,
In moments of doubt, we shall not fall.
With courage ablaze, we face the day,
Enduring the trials along the way.

From ashes of pain, we build anew,
With grace as our guide, and hope in view.
Faith's gentle touch, our guiding star,
In the sacred bond, we find who we are.

The Glow of Divine Assurance

In silence of night, His light breaks through,
A whisper of peace, forever true.
Each star above, a promise laid,
In shadows of doubt, our fears cascade.

With every heartbeat, grace flows near,
In trials faced, He calms our fear.
A gentle glow in the darkest strife,
Assurance wraps around our life.

In moments fraught, where hope seems lost,
His love finds way, no matter the cost.
Radiant warmth in our hearts ignites,
Through tempest's rage, His love invites.

Together we walk, hand in hand,
In the stillness of night, we take our stand.
A beacon bright, like a lighthouse gleam,
In each tear and joy, we find His dream.

The path may twist, but we are bold,
With faith's embrace, our hearts unfold.
In the glow of assurance, we are whole,
Divine light shines, illuminating the soul.

Embraced by Celestial Hope

Beneath the heavens, dreams take flight,
A tapestry woven with threads of light.
In sighs of the earth, we hear His call,
Celestial hope uplifts us all.

Through valleys of pain, we journey on,
In whispers of grace, we're never alone.
Each step we take, a dance of trust,
In the arms of love, our souls adjust.

With wings of faith, we rise and soar,
Embraced by grace forevermore.
In shadows cast, He lights our way,
Celestial hope brightens the day.

In every heartbeat, a promise lives,
In giving of self, our spirit gives.
Through trials faced, we stand so tall,
United in purpose, we conquer all.

Embrace the warmth of His gentle light,
In love's soft glow, we find our might.
Celestial hope, our guiding star,
Leading us onward, no matter how far.

A Whisper in the Dark Night

In shadows deep, where silence reigns,
A whisper calls, dissolving chains.
Through unending night, faith lights the heart,
Kindling the spark that won't depart.

When burdens heavy weigh us down,
In whispered prayers, grace is found.
His gentle voice, a soothing balm,
In trials faced, it brings us calm.

With every star, a story shared,
In darkened skies, we are prepared.
A whisper stirs the soul to rise,
In faith's embrace, we touch the skies.

Though doubts may creep, and shadows loom,
In hope's warm glow, we find our room.
Listening close, we sense the day,
In every whisper, He lights the way.

Cast fears aside, let courage swell,
In darkened nights, we weave our spell.
A whisper gentle, beckoning light,
Guides us through the longest night.

The Grip of Divine Mercy

In shadows deep, I seek Your light,
Your mercy flows, a gentle might.
Forgive my sins, renew my soul,
Embrace me, Lord, and make me whole.

In every tear, Your grace appears,
You calm my heart, dispel my fears.
A refuge found, in love so pure,
My faith in You, forever sure.

When trials come, I lift my cries,
Your tender voice from heaven replies.
In every storm, You are my guide,
With open arms, You stand beside.

Rejoice I do, in mercy's glow,
Your endless love, a river flows.
With gratitude, my heart I give,
In Your embrace, I long to live.

Through every path, my spirit soars,
Your holy light forever pours.
I trust in You, my every prayer,
In sacred bond, our souls laid bare.

Clinging to Sacred Whispers

In quiet moments, whispers rise,
Echoes of truth in gentle sighs.
I cling to hope, when shadows fall,
Your sacred Word, my faithful call.

The breath of dawn brings forth Your name,
In silence deep, I feel the same.
Your presence near, I sense the grace,
In every heartbeat, I find my place.

Through trials faced, I hear You speak,
In stillness found, You make me weak.
Your loving hands, they guide my way,
In sacred whispers, I long to stay.

Each prayer I pen, a song of trust,
In You, O Lord, my heart is must.
Through valleys low, and mountains high,
I cling to You, my reason why.

With every tear, a promise clear,
In sacred love, I have no fear.
Your voice, a balm to ease my strife,
In clinging close, I find my life.

The Moment of Surrender

With open hands, I bow my head,
In quiet peace, to You I tread.
The weight of doubt, I lay aside,
In surrender's grace, I find my guide.

Each anxious thought, I give to You,
In silent trust, my heart renews.
Your will be done, I humbly pray,
In every breath, Your love I weigh.

The moment comes, I feel the change,
In letting go, my soul is strange.
Like waves that crash upon the shore,
In surrender's arms, I am reborn.

With every trial, I find my peace,
In faith held firm, my worries cease.
Your steadfast love, a calming rise,
In surrender's grasp, my spirit flies.

I trust in You, my soul's delight,
In every shadow, You are light.
The moment sweet, my heart does send,
In faith and trust, I find my friend.

Binding My Heart to Eternity

In timeless grace, I seek Your face,
Eternity's love, my heart's embrace.
Through joy and pain, I hold You near,
In every breath, I cast off fear.

With threads of faith, my heart I bind,
In sacred trust, Your peace I find.
The promise held, through darkest night,
In every dawn, You are my light.

With every prayer, I weave a thread,
In destiny's path, You gently lead.
In love's great tapestry, I dwell,
In boundless grace, my heart shall swell.

The whispers soft, of love divine,
In every moment, Your heart is mine.
Together bound, through time we roam,
In sacred union, I find my home.

In every joy, and sorrow's toll,
I bind my heart, and claim my whole.
An endless journey, side by side,
In love eternal, we shall abide.

In the Realm of Unyielding Trust

In whispers soft, the heart confides,
In shadows deep, our faith abides.
With hands uplifted, we seek the light,
In trials faced, we find our might.

Each dawn unfolds a promise bright,
Guided by love, we take our flight.
With every step, in grace we tread,
Our spirits soar, where angels led.

In storms of doubt, we find our way,
Through tempest fierce, we humbly pray.
United in love, we stand as one,
In service rendered, our quest begun.

The path may twist, but trust remains,
In sacred vows, our strength sustains.
Through every trial, we shall endure,
In tranquil hearts, our souls are sure.

For in the realm of lasting trust,
We find our peace, our hearts adjust.
With open arms, we greet the day,
In faith and hope, we choose to stay.

The Stillness That Carries Us

In silence deep, a stillness grows,
Where whispered prayers like water flows.
Beneath the stars, we feel the grace,
A sacred bond in time and space.

Each moment still, the world fades slow,
In quietude, the spirit knows.
With every breath, we find our ground,
In gentle hearts, pure love is found.

The river's flow, a guiding song,
In harmony, we all belong.
The stillness calls, we heed its voice,
In calm embrace, we make our choice.

Through trials faced, the calm remains,
In faith unyielding, love sustains.
In sacred trust, our burdens cease,
In moments still, we find our peace.

For in the depths of quiet grace,
We find our truth, we find our place.
In stillness found, our hearts will swell,
In love, we know, all will be well.

Threads Woven in Spirit's Fabric

In tapestry bright, our lives entwine,
With threads of hope, in patterns divine.
Each heart a note in the hymn of love,
We are the echoes of grace from above.

Through trials faced, and joys displayed,
In every moment, together we've prayed.
With hands held tight, we weave the strands,
In unity forged, we take our stands.

With colors rich, our spirits blend,
In kindness shared, to heal, to mend.
Each story told, a stitch in time,
In love's embrace, our souls will climb.

With faith as our guide, we journey on,
Through valleys low, to peaks of dawn.
Each thread a bond, in spirit's art,
In love's great weave, we play our part.

For in this fabric, sacred and true,
We find our strength in all we do.
In life's great loom, we are the grace,
Together woven, in time and space.

Holding Fast to Sacred Truth

In shadows cast, a light remains,
A sacred truth that ever claims.
With open hearts and steadfast will,
In quiet moments, our souls are still.

Through trials faced, our spirits rise,
In every tear, in every sigh.
We gather strength from love's embrace,
In sacred truth, we find our place.

With voices strong, we sing the song,
In harmony, we all belong.
In every laugh, in every prayer,
We hold the truth, our lives laid bare.

Though tempests roar and doubts may creep,
In steadfast faith, our promises keep.
With hearts aligned, we walk as one,
In sacred truth, our race is run.

For holding fast to what is right,
In love, we conquer, in truth, we fight.
Together bound, we face each day,
In sacred truth, we find our way.

Anchored in Silent Devotion

In quiet prayer, my heart takes flight,
Guided by faith, through the still of night.
Each whispered plea, like a gentle song,
Anchored in love, where I belong.

Beneath the stars, I find my peace,
In sacred moments, my worries cease.
A spirit filled with grace so bright,
In silent devotion, I seek the light.

The world may rage, but I remain still,
Trusting in wisdom, bending to will.
In every breath, I feel Him near,
Whispering hope, dispelling fear.

With every dawn, I rise anew,
Bathed in mercy, forever true.
I stand renewed in faith's embrace,
In silent devotion, I find my place.

The Covenant of True Strength

In trials faced, our spirits grow,
A covenant formed in the depths below.
With hands united, we stand as one,
Faithful and strong, our battles won.

Through storms we march, side by side,
In the light of love, our hearts abide.
Each struggle binds us, heart and soul,
In this holy journey, we are whole.

The strength we share, a sacred thread,
A promise held, where fear has fled.
With every challenge, in trust we rise,
The covenant forged beneath the skies.

In unity's bond, we find our might,
Guided by faith, embracing the light.
Together we flourish, through thick and thin,
The covenant of true strength within.

In the Arms of Providence

Held close by grace, I find my rest,
In the arms of Providence, truly blessed.
With open hearts, we journey forth,
Embracing joy, grounding our worth.

Through valleys low, and mountains tall,
I trust the love that conquers all.
In every moment, His plan unfolds,
A tapestry rich, in colors bold.

With gentle hands, He shapes our way,
In the arms of Providence, come what may.
Each step we take, a path divine,
Caressed by grace, in love we shine.

In trials faced, we find our song,
Together we rise, forever strong.
With faith as our anchor, we sail ahead,
In the arms of Providence, we are fed.

Beyond the Veil of Despair

In shadows deep, where hope seems lost,
Beyond the veil, we bear the cost.
Yet still we rise, with hearts ablaze,
To seek His light, in all our days.

With faith the beacon, we press ahead,
Through valleys low, where doubts are bred.
In whispered prayers, our spirits soar,
Beyond the veil, we find much more.

Each tear we shed, a seed of grace,
In every struggle, we find our place.
With every dawn that breaks so clear,
Past the veil of despair, we persevere.

For love, it conquers, it heals the soul,
In unity's embrace, we feel made whole.
Together we journey, hand in hand,
Beyond the veil of despair, we stand.

The Gentle Pull of Grace

In silence, whispers call my name,
A tender touch, a flickering flame.
Through shadows dark, light breaks anew,
With every step, I am led to you.

In valleys low, your presence near,
A soothing balm to quiet fear.
With gentle hands, you shape my soul,
Your mercy flows, it makes me whole.

With every breath, I feel your grace,
In every heart, a sacred space.
You guide my heart, you hold my hand,
In love I find, I understand.

The morning dew, the evening sigh,
In fleeting moments, I draw nigh.
Your whispers echo through the air,
In every shadow, I find your care.

So draw me close, and let me see,
The gentle pull that sets me free.
In surrender, I find my way,
In love's embrace, I choose to stay.

In the Clutch of the Holy Spirit

In twilight's hush, I feel your might,
The winds of change, a holy flight.
You move within, a stirring force,
In every heart, you set the course.

Through chaos loud, you bring me peace,
In every trial, my fears decrease.
You wrap my soul in love's embrace,
And guide my steps with gentle grace.

With open arms, I seek your touch,
In your embrace, I find so much.
You lift the weight, you calm the storm,
In sacred truth, I am reborn.

In quiet prayer, I hear your call,
You're with me now, you catch my fall.
In every tear, in every cheer,
Your presence dwells, forever near.

So in this clutch, I trust in you,
With every breath, I am made new.
In spirit strong, I rise and soar,
In sacred love, forevermore.

Embracing the Unseen

In quiet moments, I close my eyes,
I seek the truths that seldom rise.
In unseen realms, faith takes its flight,
Through shadows deep, I find the light.

In whispers soft, the heart can hear,
The sacred song, both far and near.
In quiet dawn, in evening's veil,
The spirit moves, a gentle sail.

Through trials faced, when hope seems lost,
In faith I stand, I bear the cost.
In every doubt, your love remains,
A radiant light that breaks my chains.

Embrace the unseen, let it be,
In every breath, your love I see.
With open heart and hands reached wide,
In you, my soul shall safely bide.

So teach me, Lord, to trust the sigh,
In every joy, in every cry.
Through unseen paths, your truth I glean,
In sacred moments, we are seen.

The Path of Unyielding Heart

In shadows cast, my spirit stands,
On hallowed ground, in sacred lands.
With unyielding heart, I walk the way,
Each step I take, I choose to pray.

Through trials fierce, my faith shall rise,
In every storm, I face the skies.
You are my rock, my steadfast friend,
In every moment, until the end.

With every breath, your love I hear,
Through every doubt, you draw me near.
In paths unknown, my heart will trust,
In every challenge, you are just.

So let me journey, lead me on,
With unyielding heart until the dawn.
Through every shadow that I face,
I stand with faith, I walk in grace.

And when the road seems hard and long,
I seek your strength, it makes me strong.
For on this path, in love I tread,
With unyielding heart, to you I'm led.

The Breath of Assurance

In the stillness of dawn's light,
I find the whisper of His peace.
Each breath I take, a sacred flight,
In His love, my fears cease.

With every rising of the sun,
His promises shine brightly clear.
In His embrace, we are as one,
A balm for every doubt and fear.

Through valleys deep, and mountains high,
His hand will guide, my heart will soar.
With faith, I seek, and never sigh,
For in His grace, I find my core.

The path may twist, the journey long,
Yet in His light, I rest assured.
In weakness found, I am made strong,
His love, my heart forever lured.

In every trial, I shall sing,
For He delights in all I do.
His gentle touch, my spirit's wing,
In every moment, He is true.

Whispers of Enduring Love

In shadows cast by doubt and fear,
His whisper breaks the night's despair.
With tender grace, He draws me near,
In silence, love fills the air.

The gentle breeze through rustling leaves,
Speaks softly of a faithful heart.
In faith, my weary soul believes,
That from His love, we'll never part.

As stars adorn the velvet sky,
His promises hold firm and bright.
With every tear, He hears my cry,
And leads my spirit to the light.

Through trials fierce, He holds my hand,
In storms, His faithfulness will reign.
In every moment, He will stand,
A steadfast love to ease my pain.

In every heartbeat, grace abounds,
His whispers echo through the years.
With every step, His love surrounds,
A balm for every wound, my fears.

Clinging to Timeless Grace

Upon the cliff of fate I cling,
To grace that knows no bounds or measure.
With every dawn, my heart will sing,
Of love's sweet and eternal treasure.

Though trials rise like tides at sea,
His mercy wraps my soul in light.
In chaos, I find harmony,
As grace turns darkness into bright.

His promises, a sacred thread,
In every stitch, a story told.
In quiet moments, fears I shed,
For in His arms, I'm safe and bold.

With joy, I walk this path of faith,
Each step, a dance of hope and love.
In grace I find my wondrous wraith,
An echo of the One above.

When storms arise, I stand secure,
For He is with me, firm and strong.
In every moment, love is pure,
His timeless grace, my heart's sweet song.

The Still Waters of Trust

In stillness found by quiet streams,
He calms my heart, my soul's delight.
Each ripple sings of gentle dreams,
In waters deep, He brings me light.

With every breath, I trust His plan,
Beneath the skies of endless blue.
As shepherd leads, I walk with man,
Secure in faith, I know what's true.

In moments dark, my spirit soars,
With steadfast love, He guides my way.
Through open doors and peaceful shores,
In His embrace, I find my stay.

With grateful heart, I sing His praise,
For in His care, I know I'm found.
In every trial, He'll raise
My spirit high, on holy ground.

In trust, I lay my fears to rest,
For He is good, His love is just.
In still waters, my heart is blessed,
Forever anchored in His trust.

Anchored in the Divine Promise

In the shadow of grace, our hearts reside,
Where hope unfurls like wings in the sky.
With faith as our anchor, we shall abide,
Trusting the whispers of love passing by.

When storms rage fierce and doubts start to rise,
We find our solace in prayers that flow.
The promise of dawn breaks through the night skies,
In the heart of the storm, His light starts to glow.

Every tear shed, a seed in His hand,
Blooming into gardens where peace will reside.
With courage and strength, united we stand,
In the embrace of the world, our souls open wide.

Hearts intertwined in a sacred dance,
Together we walk through valleys of pain.
With each step forward, we find our chance,
To build up the broken, to heal every strain.

In the promise of love, we take our flight,
Soaring above, on wings of pure trust.
Anchored in faith, radiating His light,
Hand in hand we stand, in Him we must.

Cherishing the Spirit's Caress

In the quiet whispers, the spirit awakes,
A gentle caress that warms the cold night.
With each breath we take, a promise remakes,
Guiding our steps with a radiant light.

Through valleys of shadows, the spirit will lead,
Cradling our hearts in an endless embrace.
In the garden of faith, where love is the seed,
We grow in His mercy, adorned with grace.

The laughter of children in harmony sings,
Each note a reminder of joy that surrounds.
In moments of stillness, our spirit takes wings,
To dance with His light, where peace knows no bounds.

As rivers of kindness flow from our souls,
We cherish the spirit's gentle delight.
In acts of compassion, we find our true roles,
Spreading love freely, igniting the night.

Through trials and tears, in the warmth of His care,
We gather together, as one we will stand.
In the heart of our journey, we deeply declare,
We cherish the spirit's caress, hand in hand.

The Offering of Faithful Hands

With open hands raised, we offer our hearts,
In a world where love is a precious exchange.
Each gesture of kindness, each moment that starts,
Reflects the divine in its myriad range.

The touch of compassion, a warm, tender grace,
In our faithful hands, hope begins to bloom.
Together we carry the light through this space,
Transforming the shadows, dispelling the gloom.

In the weight of our burdens, we find our strength,
As united, we journey, our spirits set free.
Each act of devotion, a bond of great length,
An offering shared, in pure humility.

With hands that have labored, and hearts that have yearned,
We gather the dreams that the heavens extend.
In service to others, we find what we've learned,
The offering grows, as we lovingly mend.

Through trials we face, our purpose remains,
To serve with a love that knows no end.
In the offering of hands, our spirit sustains,
A tapestry woven, in grace we depend.

A Bridge Over Troubled Waters

When tempests are raging, and hope starts to fade,
We lift up our eyes to the skies above.
With faith as our guide, we will not be swayed,
Creating a bridge of unyielding love.

In the depths of despair, where sorrows may dwell,
Our spirits unite to rise from the tide.
Hand in hand we stand, where the shadows fell,
As beacons of light, we shine from inside.

Through trials and tears, reaching out in grace,
We build a strong bridge that no storm can break.
With every kind word, we find our true place,
In the heart of the struggle, new paths we will make.

As rivers of laughter flow freely and bright,
We gather the fragments of faith with our own.
In the light of compassion, we find our true sight,
Together we rise, never facing alone.

In unity's strength, we weather the night,
A bridge over waters that once felt so wild.
With love in our hearts, we reclaim the light,
Transforming our journey, forever reviled.

Milton Keynes UK
Ingram Content Group UK Ltd.
UKHW020043271124
451585UK00012B/1023